Peter Tunstall

FIRST FEATS

Cover illustration by Geoff Hocking

A Piccolo Book
Pan Books London and Sydney

First published in book form 1975 by
Pan Books Ltd, Cavaye Place, London SW10 9PG
ISBN 0 330 24087 0

Printed in Great Britain by
Richard Clay (The Chaucer Press) Ltd, Bungay, Suffolk

Contents

27 The first man to make a telephone call
28 The first airship to cross the Atlantic
29 The first men to climb Dhaulagiri
30 The first surface crossing of the Arctic Ocean
31 The first there-and-back Channel flight
32 The first transatlantic radio signal
33 The first human heart transplant
34 The first man to ride a horse from Buenos Aires to Washington
35 The first Space walk
36 The first Europeans to reach the West Indies
37 The first non-stop Atlantic flight
38 The first woman to fly solo from Europe to Australia
39 The first four-minute mile
40 The first men to climb Everest
41 The first flight from France to England
42 The first submarine voyage
43 The first man to fly at more than 1,000 mph
44 The first solo transatlantic flight
45 The first men on the Moon
46 The first man to drive at over 300 mph
47 The first men to reach the North Pole

1 The first balloon flight

The first balloon flight was made by two Frenchmen on 21 November 1783. They were a twenty-nine-year-old doctor from Metz, Jean François Pilatre de Rozier, and his friend the Marquis d'Arlandes.

The balloon was lifted by hot air – straw was burned in a brazier in the basket underneath.

Taking off near Paris, they flew about five miles right across the city, landing gently after twenty-five minutes.

Five weeks earlier, Pilatre de Rozier had made the first ascent in a balloon which was held captive by ropes.

2 The first men to fly across the Pacific

The first men to fly across the Pacific were Charles Kingsford-Smith, a fellow Australian, Charles Ulm, and two Americans: radio-operator James Warner and navigator Harold Lyons. They started the three-stage trip on 31 May 1928 in a three-engined Fokker aircraft named the 'Southern Cross'.

The first leg, from Oakland on San Francisco Bay to Honolulu in Hawaii, was uneventful – they were near shipping routes and knew the area. But from Honolulu they flew over miles of open sea, with scant knowledge of the weather and no radio beacons to help them.

And soon they were in trouble: severe storms tossed their aircraft as they fought their way to Fiji. There they made a rough landing on a sports ground. The field was not big enough for them to take off, so they had the plane towed to a nearby beach and took off from there.

It was not until 8 June that they arrived in Brisbane, Australia, 7,300 miles from the start of their journey.

3 The first voyage round the world

The first voyage round the world was made by eighteen men, remnants of an original party of 265 led by the Portuguese navigator Ferdinand Magellan.

Men from nine countries sailed with Magellan, in the service of Spain's King Carlos I. They set out from Sanlucar de Barrameda in five ships on 20 September 1519, voyaging south-westwards across the Atlantic and down the coast of South America.

Discovering the passage between the mainland and Tierra del Fuego now called Magellan Strait, they crossed the Pacific in a north-westerly direction, making landfall at Guam in the Marianas on 6 March 1521.

Disease, starvation, injury, storms and skirmishes took a terrible toll and their numbers dwindled rapidly. Magellan himself was killed in a fight with natives in the Philippines.

Led by Sebastian Elcano, one of Magellan's lieutenants, the survivors reached Spain again in the *Victoria* on 7 September 1522.

4 The first men to climb the Matterhorn

The first men to climb the Matterhorn were under the leadership of Edward Whymper, an English wood-engraver. They were seven in number: four Britons with one French and two Swiss guides.

The Matterhorn, 14,688 feet high, is one of the most daunting and dangerous mountains in the Alps. The top 3,000 feet of this horn-shaped peak are particularly difficult to climb.

Between 1861 and 1865 Whymper made six attempts to ascend it from the Italian side; each time he had to retreat, driven back by the cold and the problems of the rock.

Then on 14 July 1865, his seven-man party, which included a clergyman and a lord, tackled the mountain from the Swiss side and fought to the top.

But tragedy struck on the equally hazardous journey down. One man slipped and fell . . . dragging three of his companions with him to death.

Only Whymper and the two Swiss guides, father and son, were left, shaken, clinging to the rock – saved because the rope that linked them to their colleagues had snapped.

The first woman in Space was the Russian cosmonaut Valentina Tereshkova.

She was twenty-six when she was blasted into orbit on 16 June 1963. It was only the sixth manned Russian spaceflight, and the twelfth ever.

Already in space was Russia's fifth manned spaceship flown by cosmonaut Valery Bykovsky.

Valentina orbited the Earth 48 times in a flight lasting 70 hours 50 minutes, during which she flew the craft herself part of the time, instead of relying on ground control. Valentina came within three miles of Bykovsky's craft before re-entering the atmosphere and parachuting to Earth.

She is happily married to another cosmonaut, Andrian Nikolayev, and has a family.

5 The first woman in Space

6 The first Europeans to explore North America

The first Europeans to explore North America were a Viking crew nearly 1,000 years ago.

In AD 986, when his ship was blown off course, Bjarni Herjolfsson sighted land to the west of Greenland, then a Viking colony. In 1002 Leif Ericsson, with a thirty-five man crew, set out to find this new land. Their 75-foot ship, a *knorr* ('ocean-striding sea-bison') was as safe in heavy seas as she was uncomfortable. The crew had no shelter, no fire for cooking food, and real fears of evil spirits and monsters to add to their terrors of the unknown.

But they went on . . . and eventually reached a region of bleak flat rocks, probably Labrador. From there, they sailed south to a great river swarming with salmon, and camped for the winter on its banks. Finding fruit for wine-making, probably grapes or mountain cranberries, they named the place 'Vinland'.

Ericsson's voyage inspired other Norsemen to follow him and some stayed in America for several years. There are traces of Viking settlements in Newfoundland.

7 The first men to climb Annapurna

The first men to climb Annapurna were eight Frenchmen led by Maurice Herzog, an engineer.

Annapurna, in the Himalayas, is 26,493 feet (8075 metres) high and when Herzog and his party tackled it in 1950 no one had conquered so mighty a peak. Supported by a group of Sherpas – Nepalese tribesmen – the Frenchmen fought their way up over ice-covered rocks and great crevasses. Several times avalanches threatened to sweep away their camps.

Finally on 3 June 1950, in bitter cold, Herzog and Louis Lachenal, a ski-instructor, worked their way up the last 1,800 feet. The struggle took them eight hours.

On the way down they both suffered severe frostbite and Herzog, who had lost his gloves, became dangerously ill. He and two other climbers were also blinded by snow glare. Their colleagues helped them down the mountain in an agonizing race against coming monsoon storms.

Jacques Oudot, the party's doctor, worked frantically to save Herzog and Lachenal, amputating toes and fingers without anaesthetics.

All survived, but Herzog spent three years in hospital as a result of his ordeal.

8 The first person to fly in a glider

The first person to fly in a glider was a ten-year-old English boy, in 1853. The glider was built by Sir George Cayley who, after experimenting with small models on his Yorkshire estates, made one big enough to carry the boy, probably the son of one of the servants. A team of men ran down a slope towing the craft until it flew for a few yards.

The second 'glider pilot' was Sir George's coachman, John Appleby. Again, the glider was towed downhill until it became airborne. When it landed Appleby scrambled out, shaken, saying indignantly, 'Sir George, I wish to give notice. I was hired to drive, not fly.'

Cayley was the first man to describe the mathematical principles of flight by a machine heavier than air, to demonstrate the use of curved wing sections, to advocate streamlining and to suggest using an internal-combustion engine to power the machine.

Since petrol engines hadn't been invented then, he built one powered by gunpowder!

9 The first man in Space

The first man in Space was Flight-Major Yuri Alekseyevich Gagarin, an officer in the Russian Air Force.

On 12 April 1961, he was launched into Space by rocket near Baykonour, in Kazakhatan, about 200 miles north-east of the Aral Sea.

In the spacecraft 'Vostok 1', Gagarin made one 89-minute orbit of the Earth, during a flight lasting 1 hour 48 minutes. He landed by parachute near Engels, 450 miles south-east of Moscow.

He was the first man to experience weightlessness in Space, and the fact that he suffered no ill-effects was of great importance to future spaceflights.

Gagarin received the title of Hero of the Soviet Union and was awarded the Order of Lenin.

He was killed in an aircraft crash on 27 March 1968.

10 The first man to fly an aeroplane

The first man to fly an aeroplane was Orville Wright, an American.

In 1892 he and his brother Wilbur, both brilliant mechanics, set up a bicycle shop in Dayton, Ohio, and began building their own machines. Four years later they started experimenting with flying machines, spending all their spare time and cash on building and testing gliders. To do this they moved to Kitty Hawk, a remote part of North Carolina, and lived in a hut.

The Wright brothers had designed and built a petrol engine to fit into one of their gliders, and on 17 December 1903 they tossed a coin to decide who should make the first trip in the powered machine. Orville won.

The machine, the *Flyer*, which was mounted on a rail, ran smoothly along, rose into the air and flew for about twelve seconds, covering 120 feet.

The Wright brothers were so confident of their work that they were the only people not surprised when the machine actually flew!

11 The first European to round the Cape of Good Hope

The first European to round the Cape of Good Hope was a Portuguese, Bartolomeu Dias de Novais.

He set out in August 1487 with two caravels – light ships about 75 feet long – and a store ship. The farthest south anyone had sailed before was to Cape Cross, now in South-west Africa. Headwinds made the voyage difficult, but soon after Dias passed Cape Cross a strong offshore wind blew him out to sea.

Taking advantage of it, he kept sailing south-westwards into the Atlantic for thirteen long days, while his terrified sailors wondered where they would end up. Then Dias turned east.

When after several days he had sighted no land, he knew he must have rounded the tip of Africa. He turned north, made a landfall at what is now called Mossel Bay, and cruised along the coast for 200 miles. Then, with the route to the riches of India and the East at last open, his crews mutinied and made him turn back!

12 The first man to swim the Channel

The first man to swim the Channel was Captain Matthew Webb, an Englishman. The daredevil captain, then twenty-seven, plunged off Dover Pier at 12.56 PM on 24 August 1875, and set off towards Calais, doing a steady breast-stroke. The faster crawl was unknown then. By 11 PM a dozen of the twenty miles lay behind, and he was still swimming strongly. On he battled, fortified with strong ale and beef tea passed from an accompanying boat.

Then the tide turned against him and a breeze sprang up. The hours seemed like days as he pitted all his strength against the sea. Worse followed when a swell developed and the merciless current drove him off course, adding miles and hours to his ordeal.

With a mile to go, one of the boatmen jumped overboard and swam alongside the exhausted Webb, urging him to make one final effort.

At last, after 21 hours 45 minutes in the Channel, Webb's feet scraped Calais beach. He had done it!

13 The first men to reach the South Pole

The first men to reach the South Pole were five Norwegians – Olaf Bjaaland, Helmer Hanssen, Oskar Wisting, Sveere Hassel and their famous leader Roald Amundsen.

Amundsen sailed from Norway in June 1910 heading for the North Pole, but changed his target on hearing that Robert Peary had reached it. His party wintered in the Bay of Whales, and in the spring made a series of trips towards the Pole, setting up food depots.

On 20 October 1911, they started for the Pole with four sledges, each drawn by thirteen dogs. They knew a British expedition under Robert Falcon Scott was trying to get there first.

Hanssen nearly met his death when his sledge fell into a snow-covered crevasse. The huskies had crossed it safely, but then started fighting. The other men managed to save Hanssen's sledge and dogs from plunging to oblivion.

During the journey twenty-four of the dogs were eaten.

Reaching the Pole on 15 December 1911, Amundsen left a note for the ill-fated Scott, who found it a few weeks later.

14 The first men to cross Australia

The first men to cross Australia were Robert O'Hara Burke, an Irishman, and William John Wills, an English surveyor.

With sixteen other men, they left Melbourne on 20 August 1860, taking twenty-eight horses and twenty-six camels. They set up a base at Menindee, on the Darling River, and eight men went on to Cooper's Creek, 400 miles farther north.

Burke, Wills, Charles Gray and John King continued with six camels and a horse. For hundreds of miles they plodded through the heat, often short of water. At their 119th camp Gray and King remained. Burke and Wills walked on for three days till they reached the Gulf of Carpentaria.

The return was a nightmare of heavy rains. They had to kill most of the animals and Gray, stricken with dysentery, died.

Burke, King and Wills, barely able to walk, struggled to Cooper's Creek to find – no one. The men left there had retreated only hours earlier.

Burke rashly decided to march to Adelaide. On the way, he and Wills died. King, rescued by Aborigines, finally got back to Melbourne in September 1861.

15 The first men to climb Mont Blanc

The first men to climb Mont Blanc were two Frenchmen from Chamonix, Dr Michel Paccard and Jacques Balmat. Paccard was thirty, Balmat, a tough, boastful twenty-five.

Paccard had spent years studying the route to the top of 15,781-ft Mont Blanc, the highest peak in th e Alps, and asked Balmat to act as his companion and porter. In later years Balmat claimed he took the initiative.

They set out at 5 PM on 7 August 1786, wearing stout boots, carrying knapsacks and sticks. Reaching the lower slopes, they slept a few hours, then pressed on, over wide areas of ice, cracking ice-bridges and through soft snow.

They reached the summit at about 6 PM on 8 August and stayed half an hour before stumbling, cold and weary, down again. Stopping eventually to rub frostbitten hands back to painful life, they huddled under a rock for the night.

Next morning, Paccard suffered severe snow-blindness; Balmat's eyes were affected, too.

After the climb Balmat said Paccard was first to the top. Later he claimed the honour himself.

16 The first aqualung diver to descend 200 feet

The first aqualung diver to descend 200 feet was the Frenchman Frédéric Dumas in October 1943.

He and his friend Jacques Cousteau, inventor of the aqualung, were diving from a small boat just off France's Mediterranean coast, to see how deep they could go. They lowered a knotted rope into a choppy sea, then carrying weights to counteract their buoyancy, climbed down. Cousteau, acting as safety man, stopped at 100 feet. Dumas went on.

Suddenly he felt drunk and carefree, his ears buzzed and there was a bitter taste in his mouth. He felt sleepy and dizzy. Hazily thinking it was a pity he hadn't much exceeded 100 feet, he tied his weights to the rope and shot towards the surface. At once the strange feeling vanished.

When the rope was hauled up, the weights were seen to be tied on at 210 feet. Dumas had suffered the effects of nitrogen on the nervous system, producing a dangerous condition called 'rapture of the deep'.

17 The first single-handed voyage round the world

The first single-handed voyage round the world was made by Joshua Slocum, a fifty-one-year-old Canadian, in *Spray*, a thirty-six-foot sloop. He had been given the boat, but it was in such bad condition that he had practically rebuilt her.

Sailing from Boston, Massachusetts, on 2 April 1895, he first went east to the Azores and Gibraltar, where he refitted. Originally intending to go through the Suez Canal, he changed his mind and recrossed the Atlantic to Pernambuco, Brazil.

Running aground off Uruguay, he plunged into the sea to refloat *Spray*, forgetting he couldn't swim!

Having fought through the Strait of Magellan in a gale, he anchored near unfriendly Indians, who tried to raid the boat. But Slocum sprinkled the deck with tacks, and they retired discomfited.

He sailed peacefully across the Pacific to Samoa, then on to Sydney, Australia, before leisurely crossing the Indian Ocean to Durban, South Africa.

After several months' rest, Slocum sailed back across the Atlantic, reaching Newport, Rhode Island, on 27 June 1898 – having voyaged 46,000 miles alone.

18 The first men to orbit the Moon

The first men to orbit the Moon were the Americans Frank Borman, James Lovell and William Anders. They blasted off from Cape Kennedy, Florida, on 21 December 1968 in *Apollo 8*.

Halfway to the Moon all three men were ill. Doctors on Earth diagnosed flu, prescribed treatment, and the astronauts recovered. Then came the time to fire the rockets to put the craft in orbit round the Moon. This had to be done when they were behind the Moon – out of radio contact with Earth. Forty-five tense minutes passed before *Apollo 8* came back into contact.

After nine orbits the rockets had to be fired again, to put the craft on course for Earth. An error could mean shooting off into Eternity. On Christmas morning the rockets fired successfully and Lovell radioed 'There *is* a Santa Claus!' But the first re-entry of Earth's atmosphere lay ahead. Would the spacecraft stand up to friction at 24,500 mph?

The heatshield glowed white-hot – but on 27 December *Apollo 8* landed safely in the Pacific.

19 The first men to cross Antarctica

The first men to cross Antarctica were a twelve-man team led by Dr Vivian Fuchs, a fifty-year-old British geologist. They set out on 24 November 1957, from Shackleton Base on the Weddell Sea and travelled 2,158 miles by way of the South Pole to Scott Base on the Ross Sea, where they arrived on 2 March 1958.

Preparations for the trip took two years, and included the laying of supply bases along the route by a party from Scott Base led by Everest-conqueror Sir Edmund Hillary.

Fuchs's party travelled with six vehicles fitted with tank-like tracks, specially designed for work in snow and ice. Among the biggest hazards were crevasses – deep clefts in the ice covered with bridges of snow. Several times such snow bridges collapsed under the vehicles, which had to be hauled up to safety. Both the vehicles and the sledges they towed needed frequent repairs – including welding, which was carried out at temperatures as low as minus 60 degrees Fahrenheit.

20 The first European to cross Arabia's 'Empty Quarter'

The first European to cross Arabia's 'Empty Quarter' was a British diplomat and administrator, Bertram Thomas.

The Rub' al Khali, or 'Empty Quarter' of Arabia, is the largest uninterrupted stretch of sandy desert in the world. It was a dangerous trip, because the Muslim Arabs who roamed the area were hostile to all Christians.

After two earlier explorations of the area, Thomas set out on 1 December 1930, with a small party of Arabs who had taken an oath to help him.

The march lay across 700 miles of desert from Dhufar in the south, over the Qara Mountains, to the Qatar peninsula on the Persian Gulf. The party rode camels, and made short night-marches from one water-hole to the next.

Thomas had two milch camels with him and lived on their milk, most of the available water being brown and very salty. Sandstorms made life almost intolerable during the trip.

Thin and hungry, Thomas reached the Persian Gulf on 5 February 1931.

21 The first men to enter the stratosphere

The first men to enter the stratosphere were Professor Auguste Piccard, a Swiss physicist, and a fellow scientist, Paul Kipfer.

The 'stratosphere' is the first layer of outer air above the Earth. It begins between five and ten miles up. The air there is very thin, and the temperature is about minus 50° C (−70° F).

Piccard designed a spherical gondola in which the air pressure could be kept at a breathable level, to hang below the balloon.

Early in the morning of 27 May 1931, near Augsberg, Germany, he and Kipfer locked themselves into the black-painted gondola and set off for heights no man had ever reached. For ballast they used very fine lead shot, which they released to gain height. Despite the cold outside, they suffered from great heat, because the sun raised the temperature of the gondola to more than 40° C (104° F).

After several hours they reached a height of 51,775 feet – nearly ten miles up, and well into the stratosphere. They descended without incident.

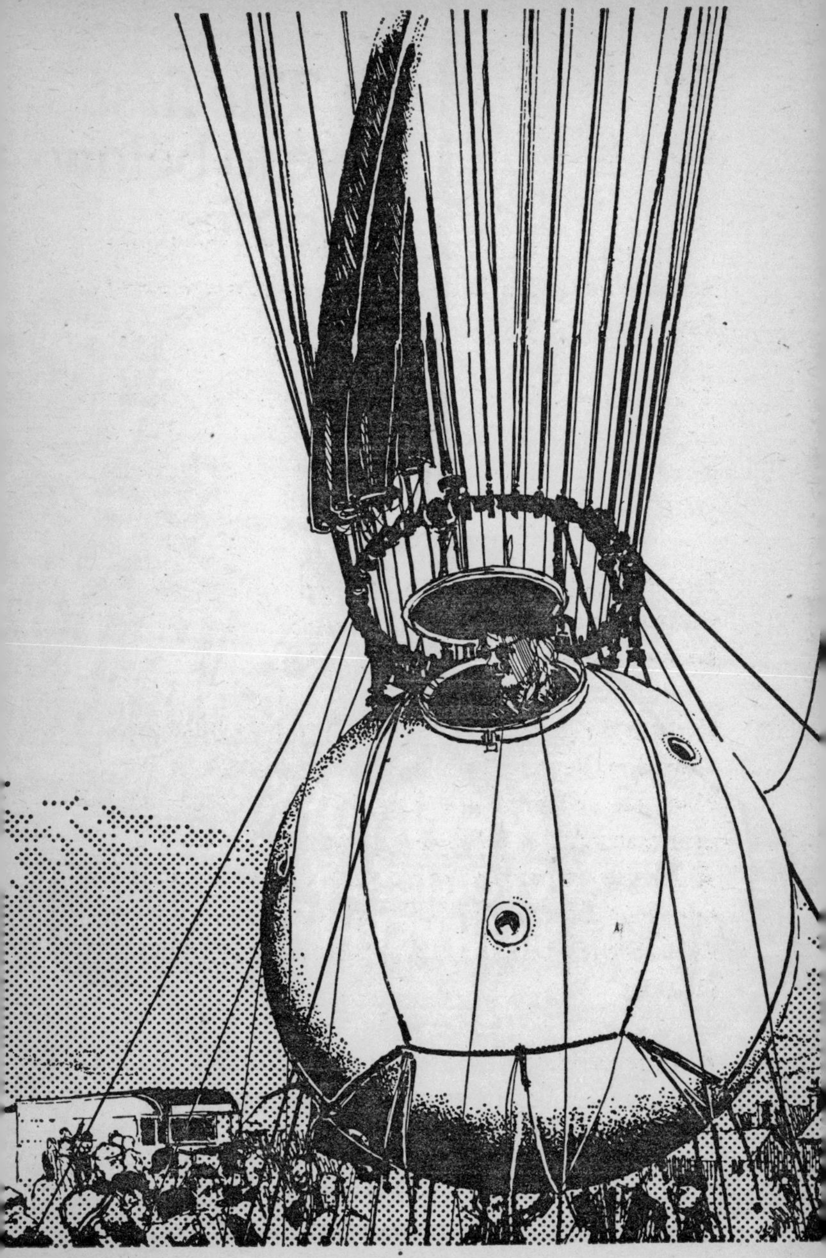

22 The first dive to below 1,000 feet

The first dive to below 1,000 feet was made by two American scientists, Dr Charles William Beebe and Otis Barton.

They made their historic descent on 10 June 1930 in a bathysphere, a steel ball less than five feet across, with walls $1\frac{1}{4}$ inches thick, and heavy quartz windows. In this they were lowered into the Atlantic Ocean near Nonsuch Island, Bermuda, on a steel cable. Telephone and power cables kept them in touch with the ship on the surface.

There was a scare nearly 300 feet down when a trickle of water came through the hatch; but it stopped. Soon they passed 525 feet, the deepest point any man had attained before, and saw for the first time the fish that live at great depths. All was well and Beebe passed the order for the bathysphere to be lowered to 1,426 feet – over a quarter of a mile down.

Forty-five minutes later they returned to the surface, having conquered a new world.

23 The first vaccination

The first vaccination was performed in 1796 by Edward Jenner, an English doctor.

In his time smallpox was a dreaded disease, which killed many people. But it had been observed that anyone who recovered from smallpox could not contract it again. Many people tried to give themselves mild doses of smallpox as a prevention – often with fatal results.

Jenner found that people who caught cowpox, a similar but mild disease common in cows, seemed to be immune to smallpox. In the face of ridicule from his colleagues, Jenner made many experiments, and finally, on 14 May 1796, inoculated an eight-year-old boy, James Phipps, with cowpox. When Phipps had recovered from it, Jenner inoculated him with smallpox – and the boy did not catch the disease.

It was a brave thing to do, for things might have gone badly with Jenner had his theory been proved wrong.

Four years later, 'vaccination', as Jenner called it, was accepted by the medical world, and smallpox began to lose its terrors.

24 The first men to cross Greenland's ice-cap

The first men to cross Greenland's ice-cap were led by the famous explorer Fridtjof Nansen. With him were fellow Norwegians Otto Sverdrup, Oluf Dietrichson and Kristian Trana, and two Lapps, Ravna and Balto.

Nansen planned to land on the barren east coast and march to the west, where there were settlements. So they had a goal – but no hope of retreat. A sealer took them close to land at Sermilikfjord on 17 July 1888, and they transferred to two small boats. But the current swept them miles south.

They had to march on skis about 200 miles up the coast before they could turn inland, which they did on 10 August. Fighting uphill through snow, ice and storms they reached an altitude of 8,800 feet on 5 September. When the slopes favoured them, they hoisted sails on their sledges.

They reached the west coast on 26 September, too late for the last ship of the season, and had to spend the winter there.

25 The first man to fly over the South Pole

The first man to fly over the South Pole was Commander Richard Byrd, a forty-one-year-old American.

Byrd organized a million-dollar expedition to Antarctica, and set up a base camp near the Bay of Whales, in the Ross Sea. His equipment included three aeroplanes.

The expedition spent the winter of 1929 in camp, living through four months of darkness. Then the planes were dug out of their igloo-type hangars and on 28 November 1929, Byrd and a crew of three set off in a three-engined monoplane, the *Floyd Bennett*.

Soon they had to cross a mountain range – but with extra fuel, food and scientific instruments aboard, the aircraft wouldn't climb high enough. Byrd made an agonizing decision – and 300 lb of food, six weeks' supply, went overboard. With only feet to spare, the plane slipped between two peaks, and made it safely to the Pole.

Lightened of fuel, the aircraft easily recrossed the mountains and landed back at base after a flight of 15 hours 51 minutes.

PIC

26 The first men through the North-west Passage

The first men through the North-west Passage were in a party led by the famous Norwegian Roald Amundsen.

Men had been trying to find a sea route round the north of Canada for 400 years, but had always been defeated by the ice and severe weather.

Amundsen set out in June 1903 in a 47-ton sloop, the *Gjöa*, which had sails and an auxiliary engine. He and his crew of six left Norway secretly to avoid his creditors!

The *Gjöa* sailed through the twisting channels between the north Canadian islands while they were still ice-free, during August and September 1903. On King William Island, about halfway through the North-west Passage, Amundsen established a base. He and his companions stayed there for two winters and a summer to make scientific studies.

On 13 August 1905 the *Gjöa* sailed again, but was soon forced to shelter near the coast west of the Mackenzie River by storms and ice. The ship eventually got through to the Pacific Ocean in September 1906.

27 The first man to make a telephone call

The first man to make a telephone call was the Scottish-born American scientist Alexander Graham Bell. He did it on 10 March 1876 after three years of hard work.

Bell and his assistant, Thomas Watson, began their experiments in 1873. On 2 June 1875, they transmitted sounds by wire for the first time from one room to another – the noise made by plucking a metal reed. The sound of Bell's voice was transmitted two days later, but Watson couldn't make out what he was saying.

The two men sweated away for eight months more, experimenting, trying new materials, making and re-making their models. Then, one exciting day, Bell spilled some battery acid on his clothes, and exclaimed: 'Mr Watson, come here – I want you!'

Watson was in the other room, but he heard Bell clearly over the transmitter . . . and the spilled acid was soon forgotten in their excitement.

The telephone had been born.

28 The first airship to cross the Atlantic

The first airship to cross the Atlantic was the British R–34 – and it made the first double crossing of the Atlantic by air, too.

R–34 was 643 feet long, powered by five 250 hp engines, and cruised at 45 mph. She left East Fortune, Scotland, at 1.24 AM on 2 July 1919 bound for New York. On board were a crew of thirty-two and a stowaway.

The fuel was calculated by weight . . . and the presence of the stowaway meant less fuel was aboard than the captain, Major G. H. Scott, thought.

Strong headwinds cut the speed, and fuel became dangerously low. So Scott planned to land 100 miles from New York, and the ground crew hastened to the new spot. Then Scott found he could just reach New York after all. He flew on and dropped a man by parachute to take charge of the landing, all the experts being 100 miles away!

The flight took 108 hours 12 minutes. The return flight to Britain, begun on 9 July, took 75 hours 3 minutes.

29 The first men to climb Dhaulagiri

The first men to climb Dhaulagiri in the Himalayas were six members of a Swiss expedition in May 1960. At 26,966 feet, Dhaulagiri was then the world's highest unclimbed mountain, and seven attempts to conquer it had failed.

The Swiss party, led by Max Eiselin, used a light aeroplane to lift men and supplies to the nearby Dambush Pass, 17,060 feet up. The aircraft also took supplies to a base camp at 18,700 feet, while the rest of the party climbed on foot.

For two months the thirteen-man team battled with storms, snow, altitude sickness and bad luck. Their plane crashed – fortunately without loss of life. Their oxygen flasks leaked and were useless. Nima Tensing, one of the Nepalese Sherpas in the team, fell forty feet down a crevasse.

But at last a spell of fine weather helped, and on 13 May six men – Peter Diener, Kurt Diemberger, Albin Schelbert, Ernst Forrer, Nima Dorjee and Nawang Dorjee – stood on the summit.

30 The first surface crossing of the Arctic Ocean

The first surface crossing of the Arctic Ocean was made by four Britons with sledges and huskies.

With Wally Herbert, thirty-four, the leader, were Major Kenneth Hedges, also thirty-four, Alan Gill, thirty-eight and Dr Roy Koerner, thirty-six.

They set out from Point Barrow, Alaska on 21 February 1968, on a first 80-mile dash across moving, newly formed ice to reach the main Arctic ice pack. But the area of moving, dangerous ice extended much farther, and proved barely thick enough to support as ledge.

On 4 July they camped on a solid ice-floe to sit out the summer melt. On 4 September they started off again, but Gill fell and slipped a disc. Back they went to their summer camp, prepared to winter there while he recovered. But the floe broke up and they had to move to another.

In February 1969 they set out again, reached the North Pole on 6 April, and finally touched land at Tavløya, Spitsbergen on 29 May.

31 The first there-and-back Channel flight

The first there-and-back Channel flight was made in June 1910 by the Hon Charles Stewart Rolls, British pioneer of motoring and flying who, with engineer Henry Royce, produced the famous Rolls-Royce cars and aeroengines.

Rolls, thirty-two, flew a British-built version of the biplane designed by the Wright brothers.

After waiting near Dover for several days for suitable wind and weather, Rolls took off in the evening of 2 June, crossed the Channel, then flew inland as far as Sangatte, near Calais.

There he dropped a letter addressed to the Aero Club of France – to prove he had made the trip – and turned back to Dover, where he landed safely. The whole trip took just over ninety minutes.

He had scored another first, too – it was the first aeroplane flight from England to France. Rolls was killed in a crash a month later.

32 The first transatlantic radio signal

The first transatlantic radio signal was made possible by Guglielmo Marconi, the Italian inventor, on 12 December 1901.

Marconi, then twenty-seven, had a transmitter at Poldhu, in Cornwall, England, and early in 1901 began setting up another radio station at Cape Cod, Massachusetts.

Only weeks before the attempt was to be made, a terrible storm shattered the masts at Cape Cod. Marconi, undaunted, transferred to St John's, Newfoundland, arriving there on 6 December with all the apparatus he needed. This time, instead of masts to carry the aerial, he decided to use a balloon. But when they set up their station, another gale blew away the balloon.

Still not beaten, Marconi sent a kite up into the stormy air, carrying 600 feet of aerial wire. Then he settled down, quietly drinking cocoa, to wait for the signals from England.

At 12.30PM they came . . . three sharp clicks, the Morse letter S. The Italian had thrown an invisible bridge 2,170 miles across the Atlantic.

33 The first human heart transplant

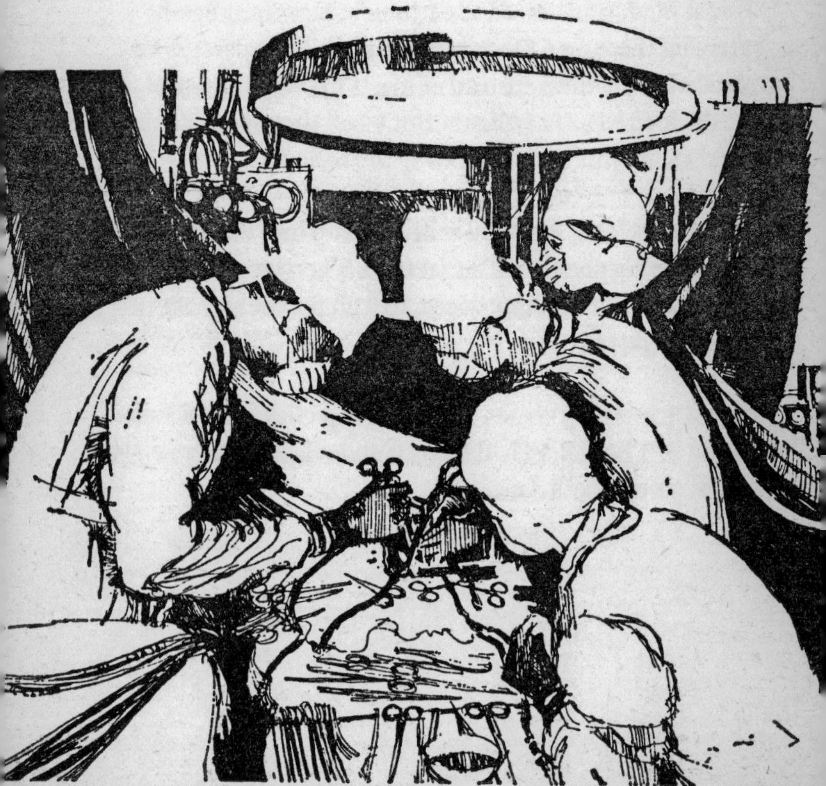

The first human heart transplant was performed by Dr Christiaan Barnard, a South African surgeon, at the Groote Schuur Hospital, Cape Town. The patient was Louis Washkansky, fifty-six, a wholesale grocer dying of heart disease. The donor, twenty-five-year-old Denise Darvall, had received fatal head injuries in a road accident.

The operation, which began at night, soon became a race against time – the donor's heart had to be used as soon as possible after death or it would be useless. Massive doses of drugs were given to Washkansky to prevent his body rejecting the new heart. But they lowered his resistance to infection.

The patient came round from the operation, and by the sixth day was feeling better than he had for years. But after five more days a massive lung infection set in, and Louis Washkansky died just eighteen days after the operation.

His new heart had worked well up to the last moment.

34 The first man to ride a horse from Buenos Aires to Washington

The first man to ride a horse from Buenos Aires to Washington was Amié Felix Tschifelly, a thirty-year-old Swiss teacher, who began this incredible 10,000-mile horseback journey on 23 April 1925. He used two horses, riding one and using the other to carry supplies.

His route lay through Argentina, drenched by rain, over the Andes – where he suffered blood-poisoning – into Bolivia, and through dangerous mountain trails and areas inhabited by bloodthirsty Indians, into the hot plains of Peru.

After crossing a 100-mile-wide desert he travelled 400 miles north by river steamer. An injury to one of his horses delayed him in Panama, but he pressed on over Death Mountain to Costa Rica, then boarded a ship to by-pass Nicaragua, where a revolution raged. In Mexico the other horse was injured. A military escort saw Tschifelly through bandit-ridden country to the US border – but he found traffic on the road to Washington more dangerous!

He reached the US capital in the autumn of 1928 – 3½ years after starting out!

35 The first Space walk

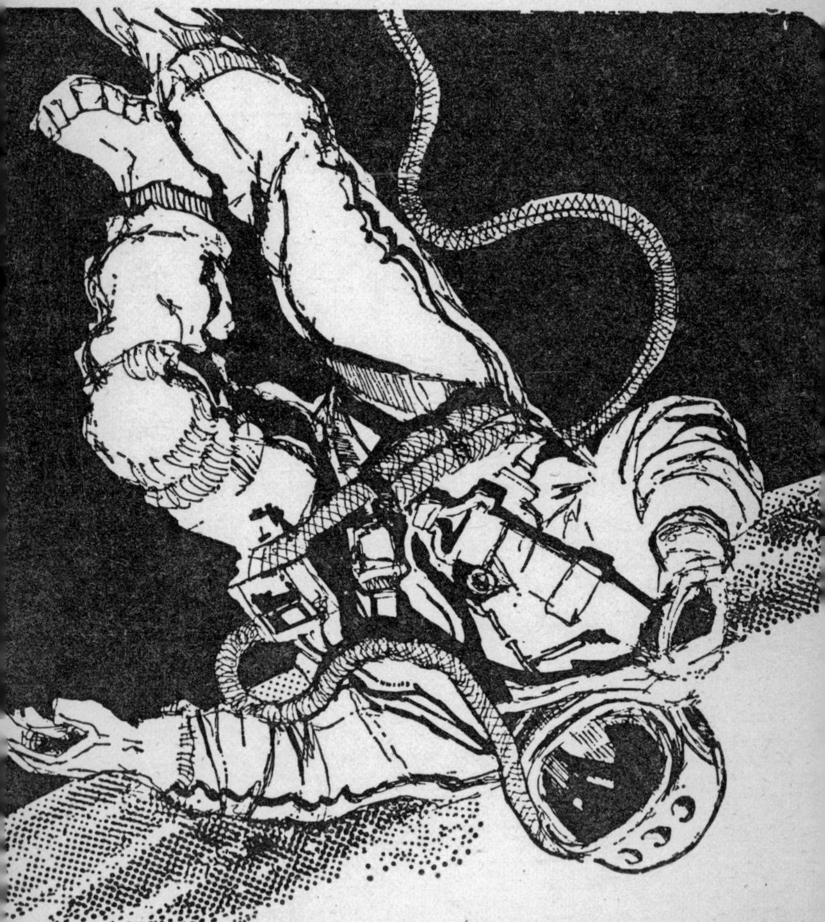

The first Space walk was made by Russian cosmonaut Alexei Leonov on 18 March 1965.

Leonov, a big, hairy pilot and artist, wore a spacesuit with its own oxygen supply. He slipped into an airlock chamber as spaceship *Voskhod 2*, piloted by Pavel Belyayev, orbited the Earth. Belyayev gave the go-ahead, and Leonov opened the exit hatch and gazed out at the Earth sailing majestically below.

Pushing himself clear, he 'swam' in space linked to the ship only by a lifeline. He manoeuvred freely, and – as he wrote later – 'saw the universe in all its grandeur'. But fatigue slowed his reactions and made getting back into the spaceship a slow business.

After eighteen orbits Belyayev made the first-ever manually controlled landing – in deep snow in the Ural Mountains.

The cosmonauts endured two days of bitter cold before rescuers could reach them – and then had to ski twelve miles to where a helicopter could pick them up.

36 The first Europeans to reach the West Indies

The first Europeans to reach the West Indies were the members of Christopher Columbus's 1492 expedition.

Columbus, a Genoese sailor, believed the easiest way to reach the East's riches was to sail westwards. Following the ideas of the second-century astronomer Ptolemy, he thought the distance westwards from Europe to Japan was about 3,000 miles – it's actually about 11,000. Nobody realized America was there.

It took Columbus eighteen years to 'sell' his idea, but Spain's Queen Isabella finally agreed to back him. He left Palos, Spain, on 3 August 1492, with three small ships – *Santa Maria*, *Pinta* and *Nina*, manned by ninety men. After calling at the Canaries to mend *Pinta*'s rudder, they sailed into the unknown for three weeks and by 10 October *Santa Maria*'s crew was threatening mutiny.

Columbus persuaded his men to sail on for three more days – and on the second day they sighted land: the little island of San Salvador in the Bahamas.

After some exploration of the islands Columbus sailed home to a hero's welcome.

37 The first non-stop Atlantic flight

The first non-stop Atlantic flight was made by two Britons, Captain John Alcock and Lieutenant Arthur Whitten-Brown.

On 14 June 1919 they took off from St John's, Newfoundland, in a converted Vickers Vimy bomber – into the teeth of a 40 mph gale.

Soon their radio had failed. If anything went wrong, they could not signal for help.

As night fell, they found themselves first in sleet, then in fog. At that moment the plane went into a spin. They came out to find themselves flying upside-down a few feet above the water. For six hours they fought with fog, sleet and darkness till dawn came and Brown could fix their position.

Six times he had to crawl out on the wings to chip ice from the engines. Finally they saw land – Clifden, in Galway, Ireland. Picking what looked like a flat meadow, they landed in a bog, damaging the aircraft.

But they had made it – in 16 hours 12 minutes, and a coast-to-coast time of 15 hours 57 minutes.

38 The first woman to fly solo from Europe to Australia

The first woman to fly solo from Europe to Australia was Amy Johnson, an English girl, in a little De Havilland 'Moth' biplane.

Carrying a spare propeller and extra fuel tanks, Amy, then twenty-seven, left Croydon Airport near London on 5 May 1930 almost unnoticed. In three days she was at Aleppo, Turkey, with the eyes of the world upon her.

Flying on to Baghdad she was forced down by a sand-storm, and had to pile luggage against the Moth's wheels to stop it being blown away.

Within six days she was at Karachi; but soon after she had to make another forced landing, damaging her plane. Repairs took two days.

In thick cloud she flew through a dangerous mountain pass to reach Rangoon. Across the Java Sea to Sumatra, bad weather gave her a rough time, and she had to make a third forced landing on the beach of a small island in the Timor Sea.

But on the nineteenth day of her 12,000-mile flight she touched down at Darwin, Australia – to a tumultuous welcome.

41

39 The first four-minute mile

The first four-minute mile was run by Roger Bannister, a twenty-five-year-old Englishman, at Oxford on 6 May 1954.

The world record stood at 4 minutes 1·3 seconds, but Bannister planned to beat it by running three 60-second quarter-mile laps, and striving to clip a fraction off the fourth by driving himself to exhaustion.

Two other noted runners, Chris Brasher and Chris Chataway, acted as pacemakers. Brasher set a blistering early pace, and at the halfway stage Bannister's time was a brilliant 1 minute 58·2 seconds.

On the murderous third lap Chataway sprang into the lead, but as they began the final 440 yards, Bannister was at Chataway's shoulder – a vital half-second behind his target.

With 250 yards to go, Bannister inched ahead and ran as if his life were at stake. In a semi-blackout he covered the last agonizing yards and staggered rubbery-legged from the track, gasping: 'Did I do it?'

The timekeepers' watches gave the answer: 3 minutes 59·4 seconds.

40 The first men to climb Everest

The first men to climb Everest were Edmund Hillary, a New Zealander, and Tenzing Norgay, a Sherpa from Nepal. Members of a British expedition, they reached the summit of the world's highest mountain on 29 May 1953.

Early in April 1953, a base camp was set up 17,900 feet above sea level, from which stores were carried higher up the mountain. The real struggle began from an advanced base at 21,200 feet. Oxygen was used by the climbers.

The first assault on the summit was made on 26 May by Tom Bourdillon and Charles Evans. Though they reached a higher point than any climbers before them, they had to turn back before night fell.

On 28 May five men battled to set up a higher camp at 27,900 feet. There Tenzing and Hillary spent the night. Soon after dawn they attacked the last 1,300 feet, cutting steps in the ice, and reached the top at 11.30 AM.

41 The first flight from France to England

The first flight from France to England was made by thirty-seven-year-old Louis Bleriot, French pioneer aeroplane-builder, in one of his own monoplanes. After being helped into the cockpit – he was walking on crutches because of a badly burned foot – he took off from Calais at sunrise, 4.40 AM, on 25 July 1909.

His engine had never before kept going for more than twenty minutes – and the cross-Channel flight was going to take over half an hour. So a destroyer followed his course ready to rescue him. There was so much mist that for some minutes Bleriot was out of sight of both destroyer and land, and couldn't be sure he was heading the right way.

Then came a stroke of luck: a shower of rain which cooled his engine, and helped to keep it running.

At about 5.20 AM Bleriot steered his frail craft down from the grey skies into a field near Dover – to win a £1,000 prize from a London newspaper and a place in history.

42 The first submarine voyage

The first submarine voyage was made by a crew led by Cornelis van Drebbel, a Dutch physician and scientist who lived from 1572 to 1634.

His boat was built of wood covered with greased leather, reinforced with iron bands, and was propelled by oars projecting through watertight leather joints. It contained tanks into which water ballast could be admitted to make the boat sink. The water was pushed out again by forcing a plate through each tank – like a piston in a cylinder – by screw pressure.

This strange craft was launched on the River Thames at Westminster in London during the summer of 1624, before a crowd of Londoners headed by King James I. It dived into the middle of the Thames, where the King from his royal barge could see it sitting on the riverbed more than twelve feet down.

Drebbel and his crew then manoeuvred the boat under water, and are said to have travelled submerged from Westminster to Greenwich – a distance of about five miles.

43 The first man to fly at more than 1,000 mph

The first man to fly at more than 1,000 mph was British test-pilot Peter Twiss on 10 March 1956. He flew a Fairey FD–2 delta-winged jet over a course along England's south coast.

For the record to be established, Twiss had to fly the course twice, dead straight and dead level. It was like flying through two invisible circus hoops 328 feet across and several miles apart while accelerating violently – and all this 38,000 feet up.

The aircraft carried only just enough fuel. The afterburner, used to reach very high speeds, had to be shut off with split-second accuracy, or too much fuel would be used on the first run, leaving too little for the second.

The record attempts, involving a team of hundreds, began on 8 March and went on for three days. Six times Twiss hurtled along the course, and six times the cameras recording the flight failed to pick him up.

Then came the seventh and last try – and an official world speed record of 1,132·2 mph.

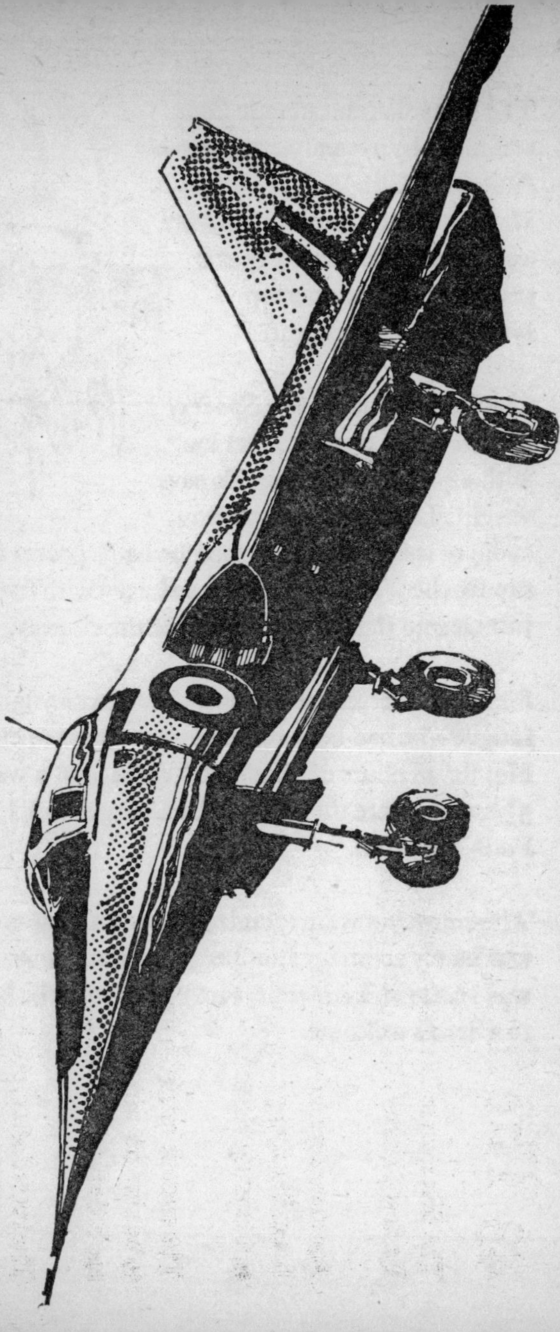

The first solo transatlantic flight was made by a twenty-five-year-old American, Charles A. Lindbergh. He took off at 7.52 AM on 20 May 1927 in a bid to win a $25,000 prize for the first nonstop New York–Paris flight.

Lindbergh's plane, *The Spirit of St Louis*, was under 28 feet long, with a 46-foot wingspan. To save weight, Lindbergh flew without radio or fuel gauges. For food he had a packet of sandwiches. Thc aircraft was so heavy with fuel that it only just cleared the trees at the end of the runway.

Soon Lindbergh was out over the Atlantic, fighting fatigue – he had been up since 2 AM after a sleepless night. Not for 28 hours did he sight Ireland, and it was another 5½ hours before the lights of Le Bourget airficld, near Paris, appeared.

The runway was surrounded by such a huge crowd there was barely room for Lindbergh to touch down safely. It was 10.21 PM, Paris time, on 21 May when he landed – to a hero's welcome.

44 The first solo transatlantic flight

The first men on the Moon were the Americans Neil A. Armstrong and Colonel Edwin 'Buzz' Aldrin, both then thirty-nine. They landed there on 20 July 1969.

With Colonel Michael Collins, they blasted off in *Apollo 11* on 16 July. Three days later, the spacecraft went into lunar orbit and after another twenty-four hours the lunar module *Eagle* separated from the command module.

There were anxious moments when the computers seemed about to steer them towards a boulder-strewn Moon crater, but Armstrong took the controls and made a perfect touchdown.

At 10.56 PM Armstrong set foot on the Moon with the words: 'That's one small step for a man, one giant leap for mankind.'

After several hours, Armstrong and Aldrin re-entered the lunar module. Then came the critical moment: would *Eagle* take off from the Moon safely? It did, and soon the two men were reunited with Collins.

They returned to Earth on 24 July after an eight-day trip of more than a million miles.

45 The first men on the Moon

46 The first man to drive at over 300 mph

The first man to drive at over 300 mph was British speed ace Sir Malcolm Campbell. He set the record on 3 September 1935, when he was fifty years old.

Campbell had made an attempt a few months earlier at Daytona Beach, Florida, but the beach was so dangerous he could reach only 276·8 mph. He made his next attempt at Bonneville Salt Flats, Utah, where conditions were much better. But a railway embankment crossed the track some four miles from the end of the measured mile over which the record runs were to be made, and there were doubts whether Campbell's 2000 horse power car *Bluebird* could pull up in time to avert a crash. Special wind-brakes were fitted, and with these Campbell was able to bring the great car safely down to a controllable speed with space to spare.

Over two runs he averaged 301·129 mph – the thirteenth time he had broken the world's land speed record.

47 The first men to reach the North Pole

The first men to reach the North Pole were led by a US Navy engineer, Robert Edwin Peary. They set out in the SS *Roosevelt* in 1908, landed on the shores of Grant Land in the extreme north of Canada, and travelled on over the ice with dog-sleds.

Initially there were twenty-five men in the expedition, seventeen of them Eskimos, but as food ran short, groups of them were sent back.

Six men reached the Pole on 6 April 1909: Peary, his manservant Matthew Henson, and four Eskimos.